Living Your Best Life Broken

Finding the Beauty in Your Broken Pieces

Pastor Patrick Diggs

Publisher: TempleXII

ISBN: 979-8-218-13600-0

This book is dedicated to my dear friend James Jones, who became an amputee after an F-250 truck hit him on February 24, 2018.

A few months earlier, James was relentlessly in prayer about his purpose in life and what God created him to do. February 24, he got the answer through a right leg, dangling from the thigh down. His calm demeanor during this traumatic ordeal inspired this book. Today, he continues to live and, most importantly, inspires more people to make an effort to align themselves with God's goals for their lives—even having experienced a broken limb.

His motto: It is not easy, but God never promised it would be. God's presence is the reward.

Thank you for your godly testimony, brother!

Contents

Acknowledgments

I cannot thank my siblings, Cynthia Diggs and Laurie Diggs of 3D Ministries, enough for not only seeing my broken process, but supporting my efforts to help God bring the complete picture into fruition. They would not accept invitations to my private pity party and pushed me to continue to live when life seemed to get the best of me. Thank you, ladies.

I also owe a great debt of gratitude to my church family, who actually feel like a real family, for trusting my story enough to listen to sermons on brokenness. I love you all with every ounce of my heart.

I'd also like to thank all the people who set out to use my brokenness to market themselves and their ministries, and I'd like to thank those who drew their own conclusions about me without knowing the real me.

I'd like to appreciate those who promised to be there for me, but quickly abandoned me when things began to fall apart on the surface. You guys kept me on my knees, taught me how to pray, and pushed me into a deeper, more meaningful relationship with the Lord. You know who you are.

~Patrick J Diggs

Intro

If I could write the perfect story of my life, it would be filled with success stories of the things I set out to accomplish. Of course, I'd be wealthy, worry free and admired by all. But the truth of the matter is that each one of us encounters failed plans, miserable mishaps, tragedies flanked with misery, broken promises and plenty of broken dreams.

We break down.

Some of us have broken a lot of things while others of us have been broken by things—things we cherished and yes, even things we loved. You can become broken by circumstances, bad decisions, poor relationships, and even by the consequences of your own actions. Others see your brokenness and can identify with and maybe even offer some help, but I'm afraid too many people, including myself, mask it with glamour, manufactured glory, and by getting our hands on a few more good things.

If you are experiencing brokenness right now, then you can identify with what I'm saying. Secretly, you feel like you've been kicked in the gut. Your life is a constant migraine headache—as if someone sawed it open and filled it with razor blades, shaking it as hard as they can.

You feel as though you are a shell of yourself, a faint shadow of what you used to be. You feel isolated and alone. No one seems to care, and no one is able to rescue you from your sea of despair. This intense pain paralyzes your heart, enslaves your every thought, and robs you of the life of joy that once brought you such pleasure.

Publicly, you put on a smile, look straight ahead, and pretend you've dealt with the pain. After all, you read the right scripture, went to Bible study, and got your word from the Lord only to discover you have not dealt with your pain at all.

You only denied it.

If you are like me, you try to avoid pain at all costs by using the world's distractions. We use distractions to deal with the stress and weight we feel. Some turn to alcohol to drown their sorrows. Others deal with the pain by filling their lives with hyperactivity. (That was me.) We will do anything we can to avoid and ignore the pain. Unfortunately, when you take this road, you never really deal with the brokenness. The heartache is still there when the artificial anesthesia finally wears off. And it always wears off.

If you sincerely want to move from brokenness to wholeness in your life's journey, then you must take courage and pinpoint your pain. You must attack your brokenness with such intensity that you will not accept depression and defeat. The key to wholeness is to find healing by a power greater than ourselves. This power exists in the person who yields their life to Jesus Christ!

This power is available through Him and is so potent, it will allow you to continue to live, strive and thrive with the brokenness still attached.

Jesus understands brokenness. He knows what it is like to be betrayed and ridiculed. He had His words twisted. He was called demon-possessed. He was tortured physically and was nailed to a cross to die as a common criminal.

He was innocent and sinless, yet died as the worst of sinners. But Jesus overcame His brokenness by being obedient to God at all times. While broken on earth, he was obedient even unto death. (Philippians 2:8) As a result, Jesus rose from the grave on the third day after his crucifixion and is alive today! He chose the road to wholeness by giving His life to God the Father and allowing God to bring healing. His being broken could not and would not stop him from living his life with purpose and surely didn't rob him of the joy he had with the Father.

Now, Jesus asks you to give Him your brokenness. If you choose to do this, then remember He does not want only your pain, He wants all of you! He wants your heart, your mind, and your strength.

The only way you can receive healing from the pain and be placed on your journey to wholeness is to give Him the entirety of your being. You follow Him as your Savior and friend—and you play by His rules. Satan wants you to believe your brokenness was meant to destroy you, but when you give your pieces to Jesus, you will find He is the King of balancing brokenness, the Prince of our pitiful pieces, and the Savior of all our shattered circumstances. Jesus Christ is the Master of our messes! You WILL find true healing and life in spite of being broken.

Are you brokenhearted in spirit today? Do you live with a broken heart? If so, I urge you to take a journey with me on how to live your best life broken. I want you to consider living your best life broken, because nothing in this entire world remains whole. Even with your brokenness, if you stop trying to hide it, you can find peace within the pieces when you give them to the Lord to use.

Jesus is a broken specialist because everything in this world eventually cracks, crumbles, breaks, fails, and falls. You have to learn how to live with the aftermath of mistakes, maladies and mess ups. However, in Jesus, I have discovered a place that you and I can live in spite of our brokenness, because God wants to use your brokenness to bring blessings through you instead of leaving you with broken pieces.

He is the potter who reshapes the clay. He is the fixer of every broken place you and I have tried to ignore. He is the only one who will bind up your broken heart and give you abundant life!

My hope and prayer in releasing this book is to help you embrace your brokenness while gathering and giving the pieces to Jesus so he can put you back together again.

Prayer

"Dear Lord, I need you to rescue me, because my heart is broken. Please bring wholeness to my life, blot out my transgressions, and bring meaning and fulfillment back into my life through these broken pieces. I surrender my broken heart to you and ask that you take control of my life now. Amen.

Intro Questions for Discussion

1. Have I been hiding my broken pieces, and if so, why?

2. What are some artificial anesthesias we use to keep us from dealing with and ignoring our problems?

3. Do I feel like I need to be healed in order to find fulfillment?

Chapter 1~The Breakdown

As I reached in the cabinet for my glass, it happened. I closed my eyes and clenched my teeth as I begrudgingly waited for the explosion. The wine glass my mother gave me, God rest her soul, was falling to the floor and in milliseconds would shatter to smithereens. My reflexes were less than stellar as I attempted to catch it before the glass fell from the cabinet to the floor. However, what I deemed a failed attempt to save this keepsake created a bizarre adjustment with in the fall. While I prepared myself for witnessing the glass' destruction, a blessing in disguise appeared. The glass didn't break well—not totally. I managed to salvage the bowl.

You see, my failure to catch the glass and save it from many tiny pieces turned out to be an unexpected adjustment, if you will, that led me to a story within itself. The tilt from my attempted catch caused the glass to hit the floor at a strange angle. The redirect of the fall, I believe, saved the most important part of the glass. The stem separated from the bowl with the base still intact.

Now I had a decision to make.

Do I trash this treasured memento, or do I figure out a reason to keep it? While pondering this dilemma, I was intrigued by the revelation lying there on my kitchen floor in broken pieces. Fragments of glass that would need to be swept up immediately before my bare feet got cut. Those small broken pieces have caused a lot of problems for people like tetanus, cellulitis and other infections, and in severe cases, amputation if not removed quickly. As I stooped down to get the scattered fragments, I somehow saw a picture of my own broken life. A foundation, connected to a stem with a detached bowl.

As I carefully collected the smaller shattered bits, tears stung my eyes and the pain of brokenness surfaced. It was a deep hurt I didn't even know existed until I began to think about it. Why was I so hurt at that moment? Maybe it was the pain of feeling like I failed my mother because she thought enough of me to leave me her favorite glass. Maybe it was the hurt of her death finally becoming a reality I never really embraced and completely processed.

I had been sweeping my pain and all the things that reminded me of it under the proverbial rug—

the kind of pain not easily healed. My heart was crushed, as if it had been stomped on, broken and discarded. Unable to progress in my work or relationships, I had become a hostage to my own sadness.

Why was I so sad?

I felt weak and desperate for hope. The pain of my past failures rose to the surface while I knelt on the floor. My mother's death, a marriage swerving out of control down the road to divorce, a dwindling congregation and a pandemic… broken glass.

I never took time to process any of these things because I stayed busy. Busy working on the next preaching assignment, busy trying to manage the church's needs, busy trying to repair everyone else's life. Everyone's but my own… broken glass.

No one enjoys the pain of brokenness. Normally it calls for a letting go of something near and dear to us, and in my case, it was my pride. Not wanting to deal with it, because I felt like my broken life would get in everyone else's way.

Pride. While trying not to think of myself, I was only thinking of myself.

Pride.

At the time, it didn't make any sense. Yet, since the broken glass, I have learned that brokenness leads to an unexpected good. The good can be found in how you handle and hurry to pick up the pieces.

Let me explain.

I consider myself a master of piecing things together. I like to feel like I have a bit of the MacGyver spirit in me. It's been a gift I used for survival every time I faced an uncertainty, and the detachment of the stem from the glass got those creative juices flowing. Angus MacGyver (for those who don't know) was a television show about a young war hero with an extraordinary knack for unconventional problem solving. He believed he could best be put to use saving lives with his "problem solving piecing things together" ability. His acumen would always put him and others in favorable situations with fearless outcomes. You've got to see him in action at least once!

Another thing you should know about me is that I have a hard time of letting broken things in my possession go. There's something in me that thinks if I had not been so heavy handed or forceful with it, it would have never broken in the first place. So I'll always try the quick fix before I completely trash anything. The reason for the glass, of course, is for wine consumption, and I must unapologetically admit, I occasionally have a glass of wine for the antioxidants, and some nights, I'll have a drink to help me think before calling it a night.

However, after a few sips, I've had bad experiences with reaching for and missing the stem. Well, after my mother's broken glass episode (which I did not trash by the way), I learned how to use it while drinking and thinking, but not without a minor alteration. Here's the adjustment. I now have to hold the bowl with my whole hand until the glass is completely empty. These days if I want to use this glass of significant sentimental value I'd have to hold it tight with all fingers and a tight grip. The adjustment created a deeper awareness, a closeness, and perhaps a more intimate encounter with my now new instrument for drinking. It has now gone from a wine glass to a handheld goblet. I'll now have to secure it and keep it close until it is completely consumed. No more sipping, spilling and missing, causing a mess that needs to be mopped from the floor or shampooed from the carpet.

It's for this reason I believe God breaks us.

Not to cause us undue pain. Not because He doesn't love us. Instead, God breaks us to bless us. His desire within the breaking process is to move us from casual acceptance into using our creative giftedness. He desires to show us how we can still function and live in spite of the breaks. This has to be a blessing, right?

Had I decided to throw that glass away, I would have never discovered how to use it another way. I could not let it go! I'd rather live with the broken wine glass, which has sentimental value, instead of living without it. Sometimes God won't take what broke you away—he just teaches you how to live a better life with it, flaws and all. That's what God does! God will break anything he can use to get our attention and find true life in Him.

God targets an area of our life we're unwilling to submit to him or let go and use it to open our eyes. Perhaps it's an unhealthy relationship you won't release. It could be laziness that's stunting your spiritual growth or a bad habit that's standing in the way of experiencing the fullness of God. The broken glass opened my eyes to future glory that will be revealed in him because of the adjustment (Romans 8:18-23).

God breaks us to bless us! He chips away anything that keeps us from finding our true life in Him. Whatever the case or the cause, our tendency is to hold tightly to the things we believe we want. We're convinced they please us by providing the joy, pleasure, and fulfillment we seek. But God knows the truth. Things will break and let you down. Only God can truly satisfy our deepest longings. All else is counterfeit to His provision.

Therefore, God selects the tools it takes to break our self-sufficiency and cause us to turn to Him. When we give up our independence, we gain a new perspective of God's plan and purpose for our lives. In this case, the broken glass moved me to write this book (creativity), worship more intensely (closeness), and make a conservative effort to stay focused in spite of the "whatever" of life.

Thank you, Lord, for the break!

Might I remind you as this chapter comes to an end that grip I held the glass so tightly with should be a reminder of how tightly God holds us to his bosom to keep us close to his heart. He does this to keep us together and to keep us from completely falling apart because the contents on the inside are of more value than the container. I like to call it His "grip of grace" that keeps me together every time I feel broken.

Prayer

God, I see through the break that you were testing my faith. You knew I didn't want to let go, but you allowed me to hold on and keep a tight grip on something you knew would lead me back to you. Thank you for knowing me and loving me in spite of what you knew. Amen.

Chapter 1 Questions for Discussion

1. What area(s) of brokenness I identified cannot be fixed by human efforts?

2. What adjustments have I made in my life that lead to a more intimate walk with God?

3. Have you discovered a creative side of yourself you would not have discovered had it not been for a breaking experience?

Chapter 2~Everything is Broken

If Bob Dylan, singer, songwriter, author, and visual artist was a Southern Baptist preacher, and used the lyrics to his song "Everything is Broken" as an intro to a sermon, he could ask the congregants for a great big AMEN! As he ticked off broken objects from strings to hearts, from bottles to bodies, we can all identify with the words. Like Dylan, life can choke us with so much brokenness.

Everything in this world is broken!

In life, sooner or later, at one point or another, everything gets broken. However, I've wrestled with this. Is being broken a good thing or a God thing, and who determines which it is?

What's so wrong with being broken? I get that some things can't be used broken, like strings, springs and other things, but what about eggs?

I'm a lover of the omelet for breakfast, lunch and even dinner! A salmon cheese and spinach omelet literally takes my breath away. However, there would never be the joy of the omelet's savor and flavor if the eggs were never broken.

There's nothing better for breakfast than an egg omelet in my estimation. An onion and cheese omelet, salmon and spinach omelet, an egg white omelet with two slices of bacon and wheat toast is to die for!

However, how an omelet begins is anything but beautiful. Spilled slimy yolk, broken shells, and the potential pending mess that will need to be cleaned is enough to deter one's appetite from making an omelet themselves. At this point, considering the work needing to be done afterward, I'd rather order from the restaurant for breakfast than go through the process of cooking and cleaning.

MFK Fisher once said that eggs are probably one of the most private things in the world until it's broken. And boy was I about to be blindsided with a spiritual lesson that day!

If you truly want an omelet the way you like it, and I did, you have to break the eggs. Eggs are useless to eat until they're broken. Unless you plan on using them to toss, they're worthless! Even when boiled, they must be cracked before consumed.

I learned through the process of preparing for this soon-to-be-eaten omelet that brokenness, or the state of being broken, takes on a new purpose and identity after the break.

The question I was about to ask and answer was, what purpose will be revealed after the breaking? How will God use me this time after he opens and breaks me? Will I be used like the eggs for the world's consumption or would God use my brokenness to help cure someone else? Would the world chew me up and spit me out only to use me and throw what's left away like the egg? Or would creativity and correction be a bi-product of me being broken?

Only the one using the egg can definitively answer this question.

If I didn't mean to break the egg, but it broke, then the broken pieces need to be fixed or thrown away, based on how and if it can be used again. However, if I meant to break it in order to enjoy it, who's to say the break was a terrible thing?

How could this be fleshed out and become relatable in my life? There has to be some meaning to this, because I cannot elude the thought of God using my brokenness in a way that brings attention and honor to him through my life. I'd discovered a lot about myself through the soon-to-be-forgotten existence of the broken egg.

It was another work-from-home day during the 2020 Coronavirus Pandemic. I gathered my eggs and necessary accoutrements to satisfy my craving for that elusive omelet. As I cracked the eggs on the edge of the bowl, a feeling of confidence came over me I hadn't felt in years. The feeling of a satisfied stomach was about to be my experience real soon. As I cracked the egg and looked at the hard, cold, lifeless shell, I saw its future as an object of satisfaction. This experience had now become the door I would have to enter through to begin living my best life broken. It was the break I needed!

Sometimes we feel like things are happening to us, when actually things are happening for us. This was one of those moments!

The prophet Jeremiah wrote, "And say to them, 'The Lord of All says, "In this way I will break these people and this city, even as one breaks a pot-maker's jar, which cannot be put back together."'" (Jeremiah. 19:11 NLV)

(***Protection***)

I had been broken for some time, but I didn't come to terms with the why until the day I made this omelet. Once I accepted within myself what I saw through the eyes of faith, the breaking I'd gone through would lead me to a life I never imagined in God.

What I saw in the break lifted me from a hard, cold, lifeless shell into a savory, selfless individual whose goal was to give others a taste of the Spirit-filled life they longed for but did not know it. My brokenness, like the egg, had layers. An egg has eight layers, but I'd like to share with you the three most of us are familiar with. The shell, the yolk and the albumen or egg white.

The shell is bumpy and grainy in texture, covered with as many as 17,000 tiny pores. The eggshell is made almost entirely of calcium-carbonate crystals and is a semipermeable membrane, which means air and moisture can pass through its pores. The shell's outermost coating helps keep out bacteria and dust. This is necessary for the egg's protection.

(*Stabilization*)

The yolk contains less water and more protein than the white alongside most of the vitamins and minerals of the egg. These include iron, vitamin A, vitamin D, phosphorus, calcium, thiamine, and riboflavin. The yolk is also a source of lecithin, an effective emulsifier. Its color ranges from just a hint of yellow to a magnificent deep orange, according to the feed and breed of the hen.

(*Restoration*)

The egg white, known as the albumen, which comes from the Latin word albus for "white", contains approximately 40 different proteins; the main component of the egg white in addition to water.

From these components, I saw how our Heavenly Father has given us His protection, stability and the information that leads to spiritual restoration no matter what we're facing. These components can all be seen in the construct of the egg.

Each layer of my life would need to be identified and dealt with in me, according to how God would use me and how I would surrender to being used.

I had been hiding behind my shell. I wanted others to believe I was as strong as Teflon, so I kept my problems within and relied on my own strength—so I thought. The strength I thought I had was the strength God had gifted me with from years prior. Only, I didn't acknowledge it. I thought it was all me and the studious deposits I'd been making from years of learning, teaching, and preaching.

In reality, it was not my strength, but strength I received from God that had been stored. He provided what I needed when I needed it from my spiritual storehouse. (2 Corinthians 12:9 NLT)

The yolk is symbolic of the yoke Jesus invites us to take on as we may get weary in laboring for Him (Matthew 11:29).

A yoke provides direction and stability for the oxen or any other beast of burden that works under the heat and heavy conditions required to get the job done. It is impossible to plow ahead for the Kingdom without the stability the yoke provides. The albumen (egg white) has the protein power required to restore the necessary nutrients that keep the body conditioned for further future use without chemical breakdowns (Psalm 23:3). In order to tap into these traits, the egg must be broken!

In the same way, the individual must be broken and be able to endure the break. I was being broken for the betterment of a greater purpose, and I didn't even see it coming!

It kind of reminds me of the brokenness found in our favorite superheroes. Whether you knew it, all superheroes, fictional characters or real people, are all broken.

Superheroes are merely broken people who have learned to master their abilities in spite of their childhood affairs and afflictions.

We'll deal with these superheroes a little later in the book. But the movie *The Justice League* highlights briefly the lives of Batman, the Cyborg, Aqua-man, Wonder-woman, the Flash and who could forget about Superman?

They all suffered from some type of broken trauma that led them to discovering their super powers. The greater cause and call for which they fight hovers over their lives thus pushing them into a life of fighting the good fight against evil.

Although God is never referenced in any of DC or Marvel movies, a higher power gifts them with supernatural abilities beyond their comprehension but at the behest of their control.

I believe God wanted to put on display through me the power of persistence amidst internal pressure. Not everyone can continue to stay the course while under tremendous pressure. This is definitely a super power (Philippians 4:13)!

During the process of discovering this amazing super power, I had to deal with the broken pieces left behind from the appetite I had for the elusive egg omelet. I had to learn how to be happy with nothing.

This proved where my heart really was. I had been fooling myself into thinking I was happy, because I had all the things I believed I needed to live a life that properly promoted the Christ-filled life. But I wasn't happy. I quickly learned (like you will eventually if you already haven't) that losing everything you love but retaining a relationship with Christ is more than enough to start all over again. When you have nothing, no one can take anything from you. Nothing from nothing leaves nothing.

Once I was stripped down to nothing, I

discovered who I really was. You'll never discover who you really are until you've been broken down into nothing.

Your strength cannot be defined by how much you can handle BEFORE you break. It can only be measured by how much you can handle AFTER you've been broken. This is the message 1 Peter 1:7-9 distinctly shares with us about trials. The author likens our troubles to the purest of gold, which only comes from a fiery refining process. Trials are divinely assigned to us to test our constructs.

The tallest buildings in the world are not given permission to be erected by the city until the soil and framework have been tested—not to mention structural design, concrete mix, wall thickness, and other safety features. This testing is paramount before people are allowed to enter and use the building. Many individuals will exit and enter the building the architect and contractors were responsible for building, but they would probably never meet.

This was critical for me to understand as I was being tested. My construct had cracks and questionable framework that needed to be fortified before I was allowed to intermingle with many lives I never planned on meeting.

The crack of an insecure parental background would need to be tested. At the age of 12, my father's death, who was a giant of a man spiritually, and then losing a mother to breast cancer when I was 47, left a parental gap that unknowingly shifted my familial foundation. Not having my father with me, when I needed him to help shape me as a man of faith, left a fraternal gap in my life that spanned 35 years.

No doubt my mother did an excellent job (in my estimation) to lead me down the path of righteousness, but there would always be tests with an incomplete grade. Only a man can teach another up-and-coming man some things.

A foundation that was once stable left me at times feeling like a parentless child. So my parental bond was broken and needed to be tested and retested, because other families, as well as my own, relied on my construct in counseling. I felt the sting of being parentless while feeling the pressure to be an awesome parent.

You never know how much you can handle until the pressure is applied. I learned, however, the same pressure that produces diamonds can also burst a pipe.

This brokenness better prepared me to serve and sacrifice on behalf of God's people only after I passed the familial test.

Better how? After the test, the mending began.

I could now be trusted with greater relationship responsibilities. I could have never prepared myself for such a great task on my own. The mending process could only take place after I passed the broken test.

God uses broken things. He'll use a broken soul to produce a crop, broken clouds to give rain, broken grain to give bread, broken bread to give strength, and broken people to do great things. We all have to go through it!

Prayer

I thank you, God, for developing my vision through tears of brokenness. Although the pain may have broken my heart, it also cleared my path to see Your very presence in the midst of the pain. In Jesus' name.

Chapter 2 Questions for Discussion

1. What have I discovered about my life that's broken and will never be put together again? Why not?

2. What parts of my broken egg (life) have I learned to keep, and which parts have I thrown away?

3. What childhood problem helped you discover your superpower in adulthood?

Chapter 3~Gimme a Break

*I will not let you go unless you **bless** (emphasis added) me.*
(Genesis 32:26b NIV)

One of the premier ways you discover the reality of the presence of Jesus Christ, and the power he makes available in your life, is through your brokenness. This isn't easy for me to tell you, because I know it is not the way we want to discover Him. We'd love it if every day was filled with hallelujah's, shouts of joy and amens, but if you've lived any length of time, you know better than that.

If you really want to see God's face, if you really want to be liberated so the beauty of the life of Christ shines through you, you have to be stripped of your own independence, of your own ability to take care of yourself. Where he strikes a blow to the flesh in such a graphic way, you have no strength left to fix yourself.

That is always where God will be.

He will block every exit you think is going to get you out of your troubles, so he alone is your resource. Self-sufficiency creates a hard shell around us that blocks the life of Christ from shining through.

We are raised to be self-sufficient, taught to be self-sufficient. We glory in our independence, and that may be ok for people's approval, but it is frowned upon by a Holy God. If God is trying to break you, a change of address, changing jobs, changing mates won't stop it. He will use that new mate to break you down! He will create conflict on your selected career move.

It's like running away from a lion into a bear! One is not better than the other when it comes to God breaking you. While He's well known for laying his sheep down in green pastures (Psalm 23), sometimes he won't let you sleep, but instead keeps you up all night trying to make sense of the fragmented pieces of your life.

You'll leave your prayer closet saying to yourself, "I wish God would give me a break." And that's exactly what He does.

When you say, "I want to see his face," because you're tired of looking at his back, you are telling him to break you.

The Bible speaks to this over and over again, but the story I like the most is the one of Jacob and the mystery man in his dream.

Quick Exegesis (interpretation of text)

Jacob was known as a trickster, a deceiver, and very manipulative. He could talk himself out of anything.

A slick talker, his linguistic prowess put him in places others would have to purchase a ticket to attend. He was a silver-tongued assassin who could sell anything to anybody if he had the chance to make a sales pitch. He could sell sugar to a cake, shoes to a snake. He could sell wind to a kite or a left to a right. The gift of gab was his go to while the gifts given by God were buried and hidden.

I can relate to Jacob's story because I too was once a deceiver—before one night when I discovered the God I know now in a wrestling match similar to Jacob's. I had gotten spoiled by serving a God who spiritually and faithfully Fed Exed my blessings. I'd gotten my way with how I served and prayed. It seemed obvious God was pleased with me by how quickly He answered my prayers after I said amen. So I thought.

The friends I had at the time would never admit it, but I believe the stories of how blessed I was seemed a bit arrogant to them. I was blessed and had no problem letting them know. The big house, cars, and a marriage that was working was enough to puff my chest out and boast a bit.

However, I wasn't being true to who I was. I

wasn't really happy in my marriage, and the material blessings I had were not helping solidify my inner peace. At turmoil within, I masked it with the blessed and highly favored phrases I recited when others were around.

As you and I journey through life, you'll discover this to be true. Things that tickle your fancy will never take away internal pain and the ongoing problems that may torment your soul.

The one thing I knew to do was hand God my brokenness, and to my surprise, he showed up! But not the way I expected him to.

Up to that point, **2020-2022** felt like one big wrestling match, lasting for years. I'd wrestled with the death of my mother. I'd wrestled with a dwindling congregation during a Pandemic. I'd wrestled with isolation from a separation that led to another divorce. I'd wrestled with canceled plans and stalled dreams, and I'd wrestled with finding my place in the ongoing struggles for racial justice in our country.

In the midst of all of this, I wrestled with how to maintain my spiritual practices and a consistent prayer life with a seemingly distant God while chaos seemed common. I wrestled with God, yet I'm still alive to tell you about the encounter.

This is why the story of Jacob is one of my favorite stories in the Bible. Jacob was allowed to wrestle with God and live to tell about it, but not as Jacob the deceiver. The match gave him a multilayered lesson and a noticeable limp. Only God could do this, but it would come at a cost I wasn't quite ready to pay.

What I learned, however, is that you cannot choose the providential hand of God. He orders different lifestyles and paths for each of us. Some of us are given prosperity, while others have to struggle to make ends meet. Some of us have children who graduated summa cum laude, while others have to scrape up money to pay a bail bondsman.

The same God that can make you shout with joy will, at times, leave you shaking your head, crying in confusion. The key to managing these emotions is to learn how to live with a limp, which means learning how to make adjustments in a world that constantly changes. I don't understand Him, and to be honest, sometimes, I don't like it!

Jacob was running left alone at night, and a man shows up and starts a fight. We discover it to be God, but at the time, Jacob did not know. God shows up in human form to wrestle with Jacob. For no rhyme or reason, God starts a fight? God just shows up to fight? I prefer the God who says, "Come unto me all ye that labor and are heavy laden, and I will give you rest." (Matt. 11:28 KJV). I want the God who leads me through the valley and lays me down quietly in green pastures. I don't want the God of the WWE.

While we don't prefer this God, who among us has not found themselves in a struggle with Him?

God initiated a season of uncertainty and Jacob didn't truly know God. Surprisingly enough, God did not get the three-second count and pin Jacob to the tarmac for the win. However, he did not lose the match either.

When the MAN realized he couldn't prevail against him, he touched the hollow of his thigh and put it out of joint. (Genesis 32:25) We serve a God who can move mountains, but he couldn't beat Jacob? So when God realizes he can't beat Jacob, He breaks his hip.

Wait a minute! A God who breaks hips?

Yes, because we serve a God who blesses and breaks.

But why? Why did he pick a fight to lose and leave Jacob with a limp?

For the same reasons he fights with us.

1) Submit and surrender

What kind of struggle can you be in with God and seemingly stand toe-to-toe with him? The only struggle you can win is a struggle to submit or surrender your will to his. God will not make you surrender, but he will break you in order to give you a chance to submit to his will.

God says, "If I have to break your hip to make you surrender and stop fighting me, I'll do it."

Remember, he will lead us to still waters, but he'll also make us lie down.

After God breaks Jacob's hip, he's no longer **fighting God, but holding on to God.** That's exactly where God wanted him to be in the first place.

God knows how to break you!

He breaks us to get us to surrender, because we don't surrender when we see the light. We usually surrender once we feel the heat!

2) He breaks us to deepen our desire for God

When God shows up to Jacob, he shows up as a man. If he would have showed up as an angel, Jacob would not have fought him. I believe his immediate response would have been fear like everyone else who met face-to-face with an angel. Admit it. You would not be in a fight with God if you knew it was God initially, would you?

Jacob thought it was Esau. He was sleeping and someone jumped on him. Already running from his brother, he blindly believes Esau caught him sleeping.

Jacob had a problem discerning God. He didn't realize it was God until his touch broke his hip because man can't do that!

We also think we're fighting other people and

forces until we are left with a limp from the battle. Jacob was touched in the socket of his thigh so that it was wrenched out of joint.

The thigh is the pillar of a man's strength, and its joint with the hip is the seat of physical force for the wrestler. Let the thigh bone be thrown out of joint, and the man is utterly disabled. Jacob now finds this mysterious opponent has wrestled from him, by one touch, all his might, and he can no longer stand alone. Without any support whatever from himself, he hangs upon the conqueror, and in that condition learns by experience the practice of sole reliance on one mightier than himself.

This is the turning-point in this strange drama. Jacob now feels himself strong, not in himself, but in the Lord, and in the power of his might (Ephesians 6:10).

What follows is merely the explication and the consequence of this bodily conflict. So Jacob says, "If you're going to break me, you have to bless me."

Whenever God breaks you, there will always be a blessing. God would not take you through all you went through without leaving you blessed!

What is the blessing Jacob desired?

Previously, he always wanted **things:** a) Esau's birthright b) Isaacs inheritance c) Rachel's hand in marriage, these are **Things.**

But now Jacob has a new identity, which is

what he really desired but hadn't discovered yet. You can see this to be true by the question he asks after the battle., "Tell me your name." (Genesis 32:29). He even adds please to the request.

What Jacob asked is what we all should be desiring—a deeper knowledge of our God.

Like I said earlier in this chapter, the cost of a deeper, more fulfilling life in God requires a price paid in broken pieces. Brokenness is always the beginning of the blessed life!

Be careful how you judge someone's limping season.

Their being broken might be the beginning of their birthing season. Jacob didn't win that night, but Israel did. How? By leaving the person he was in the battle with God and embracing his new identity limping, living, broken but blessed.

Who you will be is always greater than who you were.

When God changes your name, he changes your narrative.

When there is a breaking. there will be an awakening.

3) A new identity

Every time he also changed their name, thus giving them a new identity.

The name change from Jacob to Israel is significant in that he went from a man who allowed his fleshly desires to reign supreme to being an individual who replaced his will for God's will. The name Jacob means "deceiver," but the name Israel translates to "let God prevail." Afterward, no one ever called him by his old name, which reminded him of his old nature.

This wrestling match was crucial to him living his best life with a limp, because he would no longer struggle with an identity crisis. It would serve as a constant reminder of how his best life would be lived after being broken. The **wrestling angel** gifted Jacob with a limp—a permanent reminder of his encounter with God.

Jacob's final glory was that he learned to lean not on his own understanding. (Proverbs 3:5)

Making contact with God comes with a price! You wanna get close to God? Get ready to live with a limp. If you are living with a limp, the good news is that you've been touched by the Lord God Almighty! HALLELUJAH!

Now go ahead and start living with your broken self!

Chapter 3 Questions for Discussion

1. What struggle do you believe God has given you to get you to grow and then let go?

2. Why is it so hard to let go of things we know are hindrances?

3. If God had not given me this limp, I would have never discovered _______________ about myself.

Chapter 4~Break Yourself

I was told by one of my college professors to study the Bible with all of my senses. To think it, hear it, smell it, and get it into my mind. So when I first read the story of the woman and the alabaster box, I smell fried chicken, collard greens, macaroni and cheese, flanked by fresh dinner rolls baking in the kitchen after a Sunday morning church service.

Surprisingly, over the smell of chicken arises this scent of some obviously expensive perfume. Nothing like the colognes I wore back in the day when cologne was in high demand, like Drakkar Noir, Polo, or Cool Water. But something like Chanel #5 or Yves Saint Laurent fills the air and changes the entire atmosphere in the room. A perfume that expensive and with that kind of influence would be the type of fragrance I'd do my best to preserve for a special occasion.

Like I told you before, I have a hard time parting with things to prolong the relationship with whatever it is I may want to hold on to. I would use it sparingly. I squeeze the toothpaste slightly, only to get enough on my brush in the morning so as to save a trip and time by having to buy more too soon. It sounds a bit phobic doesn't it? But I was raised in the era of *"waste not want not,"* and I must confess, I take side with the disciples who lamented about such a waste more than I'd like to admit.

The expensive perfume that invaded the room that day should have been saved for a special occasion right? This way of thinking is exactly why God told me in my season of sparingness to "BREAK MYSELF." The Bible teaches us that when we give sparingly we will also reap sparingly (2 Corinthians 9:6), and I believe I had fallen victim to the sin of stingy service. I wasn't blatantly withholding from God, but I noticed times when I was guilty of giving the bare minimum in serving the Lord. I, too, was guilty of giving according to how I felt I had been getting.

In my private moments, I saw in me what I didn't like to see in others. I was guilty of using the Pandemic as an excuse to do my very least while expecting God's best. If you're reading this chapter openly and honestly, you fell victim too.

We were told by our government officials and the CDC to stay home, keep your distance if at all possible, and please, wash your hands and wear a mask. Amid the chaos of Coronavirus, complacency set in by no fault of my own, but this story of the alabaster box convinced me that what Satan meant for evil God can use for good (Genesis 50:20)

Most of the woman's story is lost to time. Her name isn't given. We don't know her life story. We don't know what brought her to this moment. Matter of fact, she never even says a word.

What made her approach Jesus? What made her pour this costly bottle of perfume? Why anoint his head, and more importantly, why did Jesus allow it?

Her encounter is a short nine verses. The impact is mysterious and eternal.

Her actions represent a picture of love, service, and sacrifice. I should be taking the side of Mary based on what I know now, but if I was there when it happened, I'd be saying, "Girl that's a year's worth of wages."

I'm trying to make sense of her sacrifice. Why was she wasting it?

When it is time to make a commitment to God, our scale of values must be clear. She doesn't care what they're saying or thinking. God is not going to bless you with your best life based on what other people think. God blesses you and I according to how we see ourselves when standing in his presence—filthy rags, sinful stewards, passive attendants who at times are apathetic, lazy and self-reliant.

I wasn't completely doing all I knew to do, and I had to remind myself I wasn't here to impress people. I was created to worship God. The breaking was an obvious blessing in this case. The breaking of bad habits. The breaking of bad intentions. Anointed of God but apathetically accomplished. I would have never reached the height of knowing God through worship the way I've learned by handing him my leftover spikenard! He deserves the best and the firstfruits of all I have been blessed with.

If Jesus died for me, the least I can do is think outside the box AND BREAK MYSELF.

Break yourself is a term usually used by people who excuse the term, but call themselves gangsters or gangbangers in the urban community. These individuals have made plans ahead of time to take your belongings (usually at gunpoint) and make it their own. the only opportunity they will give you to make the right decision and give it up is to "BREAK YOURSELF" and let it go.

They're giving you an opportunity to give it up at gunpoint, or they'll take it along with your life.

It's sad and a breach of the law, not to mention disrespectful and degrading. This behavior deserves prosecution to the fullest extent of the law, but hidden deep within this phraseology is a theological principle we all should observe.

The principle is this—we all should be willing to part with anything we deem valuable the moment we are in the company of Jesus the Christ!

However, Jesus never commands us to do anything for him at gunpoint!

He stands at the door and knocks… (Revelation 3:20)

Jesus says to us today, "As you look over your life and weigh it against all I've done for you, you ought to willingly break yourself! You ought to willingly give up something to me and for my cause based on what I've done for you."

See, there are times when the Lord has to break us, but there should come a time in your life when you should break yourself. Think about it.

Don't we give to those we love? Isn't giving your best the correct response to those you love?

This woman crashes the party and breaks herself in front of Jesus and everyone there. I don't think you understand the scene as it unfolds in Simon's house that day.

They were in the house of a wealthy man and there's Jesus reclining at a feast in his honor sitting among the teachers of the Law, religious leaders, and perhaps a few other well-educated curiosity seekers, dressed in their Pharisee finest, surrounded by elegance, fine dinnerware, white tablecloths, cloth napkins folded so they look like Levite priests marching toward the Temple. Even the dirt floor had been swept…it's all proper and respectable.

Then she comes in. The room grows still as her silhouette darkens the door. She obviously doesn't belong there. Cutoff jeans and a dirty T-shirt per se, carefully and cautiously approaching Jesus. Although no one said it, they're all thinking, "She's not supposed to be here"!

She stood behind him at his feet, weeping, her tears falling on his feet. It's a breathtaking scene!

In the place of reverence and respect, standing behind him weeping, tears pouring from her eyes gasping for breath between sobs. Embarrassingly searching for a towel to wipe her tears, she finds none. So she takes the locks of her hair and desperately laps up the teardrops with kisses as she is overcome by a rainbow of emotions—fear, frustration, shame, guilt, and yes, even love.

Suddenly, she produces an expensive jar of perfume housed in an alabaster jar, not that expensive, but a simple piece of reddish and yellow pottery made of lime. From it she pours an oily perfume. This fragrance, like the honor shown Jesus here, fills only the space between the heart broken and the One who is able to mend it.

It's cheap cologne from a piece of pottery, but you cannot know the cost of the oil in her alabaster box. Simon couldn't understand it, the Pharisees couldn't understand it, and neither can you and I.

While others saw a sinner, Jesus saw a soul that hated what her sins turned her out to be. Her act of worship speaks to us today, and it speaks in a voice similar to the voice crying in the wilderness. (Mark1:3)

The voice tells us why she breaks herself.

What others deem a waste the Lord declares worthy.

She "broke the box."

This vivid act brings the manner distinctly before our eyes in order for us to see ourselves. The word implies not so much the breaking of the neck of the jar or flask, but crushing it in its entirety with both her hands.

Expensively sealed with wax to preserve the scent and keep the contents pure and unspoiled, to use it, the seal or neck had to be broken. Once broken, the container could never be used again.

The alabaster box of perfume was her most valuable possession. Once broken, she could never put it back together. It laid bare, open and exposed as a worthy sign upon the recipient.

When you and I gather in the presence of the

Lord, the breaking open should come from a place in our hearts no one deserves but our Savior Jesus Christ. Complete transparency and willingness to give Jesus our everything will seem like a waste of time to those who truly don't understand why one would serve him in that way.

A lot of things don't make sense to the average spectators in our lives who watch as we serve the Most High God.

Spectators will always speculate when broken people lay prostrate before the Lord, but the unnamed woman realizes what true worship means. It's the breaking of ourselves that gives us the joy in life Jesus brings. If her sacrifice, or anyone else's sacrifice, causes you to trade a moment of worship for a cutting criticism, you are a spectator who knows not the meaning of a broken self, a contrite spirit, and a heart ready to live and love.

But when you've carried the weight of the world on your shoulders for a week…

You wanna lift those hands and release those heavy burdens.

When God has constantly made a way for you…

You'll come to church when you don't feel like it

When God has given you the best he's got, you don't mind giving him your hands!

For this woman, it was the ultimate act of love. Why did she break herself?

When the weight gets too heavy let Jesus carry it

This scene takes place during Passover. It happens between the scheming from chief priests and the betrayal of Judas. Right between death and betrayal is a story of worship.

Perhaps she was like so many others who understood Jesus. She was used up, sealed up, and tired of using the sweet smell of the perfume to cover up what she had been doing.

She was a woman of the night who used perfume to cover her tracks. She was actually tired of her alabaster box because of why she had to keep using it! She finally came to grips with herself, face-to-face with her hurt. Being used by men, cracked in places she couldn't speak of, she breaks open her box and says by her actions, "No longer will I be used by men, I want to be used by God! Here's my best!

"I anoint you as my king! Not my boo, not my babies' daddy or late-night hookup. I crown you my king." She's a woman who is tired of carrying the weight of her brokenness alone.

How about you?

Your broken life has substance if you use the time you have to cast your cares upon the Lord (1

Peter 5:7) and let him use the broken pieces to help you build a better life.

Why did she break herself?

Why aren't you worshiping the King like me?

No one else in the room saw the significance of the moment. By all accounts, she should be angry with them.

"Why aren't you worshiping him like I am?" I imagine she'd be saying that. Her actions speak volumes to us when we miss the moment to worship because we're being judgmental.

"Do you realize who you have in your presence?" she would ask, if she was speaking.

The disciples were too familiar with Jesus, so they devalued true worship. He had to show up as a ghost to get their attention! There are times in our lives when we fail to worship Jesus due to the distractions in our lives. When Jesus shows up unannounced, we think he's a ghost! You'll never be fearful when life breaks if worship is a lifestyle.

I wish I knew more about this woman spoken of in John 12:2-3. If I knew more about her experience, maybe I could understand her extravagance.

However, I have my story of an extravagant worship experience. It's the day you decide to put everything that competes with true devotion out the front door with the trash and trade it for the treasure of Christ's love. Somehow the woman knew something we don't know.

She fills the room with an aroma, wipes his feet with her hair, makes a decision to sacrifice, breaks herself, and humbles herself giving us the steps necessary to live the best life by breaking herself.

She knows that if you humble yourself before the hand of God, he will exalt you in the presence of men.

Thank you, Mary, for not only showing us the best use of our time and the best use of our treasures, but for forgetting yourself and showing us the gospel.

If Mary was here today, I think she would say the perfume she gave that day was not a sacrifice, but what Jesus did on the cross was.

You won't mind giving God your best when he has been good!

Chapter 4 Questions for Discussion

1. What gift have you wasted on others before you saw how valuable it was when you give it to Jesus?

2. Have you ever been influenced to hold back something because others didn't see it's worth?

3. What do you have to offer to Christ that you haven't given because you feel broken?

Halfway point

I'd like to consider myself a slightly below average runner. I took a liking to running a couple of months after I started pastoring and found it to be quite therapeutic. It gave me time to sort out my thoughts and figure out my frustrations with the movement of pavement under my feet.

In my early 40s I'd usually run anywhere from six to twelve miles a week. Now, since I've turned the big 5-0, my time and my tendons will only allow me to do three to six miles a week. I still manage to get out there and run. I have to constantly remind myself the Lord still orders my steps, but I control the stride. The great news is I'm still running!

I like using the Nike run club app, because it accurately keeps me engaged with the competition in my age group and gender. When I get through half of my projected run goal, the audible prompt through the app encourages me by giving me the "halfway point" alert. It gives me the details on my current run progress average pace, time elapsed, and calories burned. This allows me to re-access my projected outcome, do a self-check to determine how I feel, and make the necessary adjustments required to finish at or above my goal.

Well, we're at the halfway point of this book, and I'd like to feel, so far, it has managed to peak your interest enough to continue reading. I hope so. I'd hate for all this writing, research, and effort I've put in was a waste of your time and only qualified me to be nominated for the "master of minimalism" award.

I've said a lot, opened myself up for extreme criticism, and uncovered many of the flaws I feel have shaped me into the person God created me to be. If you can relate to any of the quotes, colloquialisms and character flaws I've put on display, please keep reading.

Living your best life is only a few more pages away. Thank you for taking the time to stay with me this long.

Chapter 5~Broke-ology

"Therefore, we do not lose heart, but though our outer man is decaying, yet our inner man is being renewed day by day.
(II Corinthians 4:16 NASB)

The world places a priority on inner peace. It also offers thousands of suggestions to those who seek "peace of mind and soul." Usually, the gurus of inner peace point to oneself as the source of peace, and if we need any help from outside of ourselves, worldly wisdom says it will come in the form of a "spirit guide" or perhaps some crystals or herbs. The problem with such advice, besides its endorsement of witchcraft, is that it completely ignores the source of true peace—the Lord Jesus Christ.

I believe we all want to be whole or complete in every facet of our lives, because it indicates to others what the standard should look like. Listen to the people who use phrases like "I'm blessed, or I'm highly favored." In essence, they are telling you this is what the best life looks like. Their statements say, "Hey! Take a look at me. I'm healthy, I'm here, and I'm whole!"

On the contrary, if this is the case, the first thing we need to do is redefine success and what being whole looks like. What does being whole feel like? Can anyone know what a genuinely happy person looks like, and if so, how can this life be seen and fleshed out before others?

Better yet, what does God say about wholeness and brokenness? You find the similarities to be astoundingly compelling. The word whole as a noun means "a thing that is complete in itself."

I can argue that being complete, in itself, is a result of being broken, and I'll make an attempt to convince you here in a couple of minutes.

Of all the times I've experienced brokenness in my life, I've never suffered the pain of a broken bone. A hairline fracture in my ankle and wisdom teeth pulled, but thankfully, no broken bones.

Next to teeth, bones are the hardest structures in the human body. While we perceive them as rigid, bones do "give" a little when physically stressed and can even break if stressed too much. With some types of bone breaks, a bone can actually shatter to pieces.

A disease like osteoporosis or cancer can make a bone more fragile, which would make it more prone to frequent injuries like fractures.

Some fractures are very **painful**, with either a deep, intense ache or a sharp **pain**. Children who get small fractures may not experience any **pain** and may not even realize they **broke a bone. In order** for a broken bone or fracture to heal, the bone must be reset and then kept in the correct position and protected until it's completely healed.

Soon after a fracture occurs, the body acts to protect the injured area and forms a protective blood clot and callus around the fracture. The fracture then closes, and the callus is absorbed. Depending upon the type of fracture, this healing process may take up to a year.

I admit I'm a bit intrigued with osteology, the **study of bones,** and the branch of anatomy or physical anthropology that deals with bones known as bone-ology.

Many fields of science, history, and geography are given unique names to define specific branches of knowledge. For instance, biology, psychology, and sociology are all unique branches of scientific study. While the individual subject matter of each branch may differ, they can all be identified by a root word ending in the suffix -*ology*. Similarly, the individuals who learn about or practice each subject matter can be identified with the suffix -

ologist.

With that being said, I consider myself a broke-ologist. Because of my frequent breaks (some self-inflicted) and familiarity with being broken more often than I care to remember, I have declared myself an expert in "broke-ology." I have no degree in broke-ology. I have logged zero hours in the classroom of broke-ology, but I've been taught brokenness in Christ by the School of Hard Knocks.

I've spent most of my life admittedly broken, and I'd like to share my discoveries in hopes of getting you the elusive place of peace I've found deep within myself. I really want you to come to grips with the reality and revelation that your brokenness was never designed to be cured. God the Father "gifted" it to you as a method to be managed and a tool to help you mature.

Brokenness is not a disease like **osteoporosis, but rather** a condition that, if handled properly, will always cause you to lean not to your own understanding and teach you how to trust in the Lord.

Your brokenness was divinely given in order to help you grow in the grace and knowledge of our Lord and Savior Jesus Christ, so the sooner you understand this, the sooner you can begin to live the life you're supposed to be living.

There are four phases of broke-ology you'll

need to get a handle to prepare properly to live your best life broken.

Break, broke, broken, brokenness.

According to Merriam-Webster, the word break has several definitions: used as a verb, it means to separate or cause to separate into pieces as a result of a blow, shock, or strain, to crush the spirit of, to make tractable or submissive: to render inoperable.

As a noun: an interruption of continuity or uniformity, to stop or bring to an end suddenly, to bring to attention or prominence initially.

Once the roller coaster ride called "My Life" stopped or slowed down enough for me to get off, I looked at it as a defining moment. After seeing so much of myself in the truth of this word, I adopted this definition as my condition. My life experienced a break as a noun and a verb! It was interrupted and brought to a complete halt by the hand of God.

The noun break stopped me as the verb break began working its way through me. *I was literally being broken into pieces by a blow from God that shocked my system and crushed my spirit. It taught me, and is still teaching me, how to surrender and bring under submission my will to the will of God.*

God is doing the same thing to you at this very

moment. If the noun break has made a positive difference in your walk with God and has made you more sensitive to His voice, then the verb break is the Holy Spirit and the breaking is doing its job.

The method of breaking a horse is worthy of explaining here. As big and powerful an animal as a horse is, they can be controlled with a small piece of metal and a few leather straps. How can this be? Well, it's because the horse has been broken. There's a wide range of techniques that can be used to break a horse and the same methods can be used on human beings.

The different stages of breaking a horse.

1. **Unbroken**

    During the unbroken stage, the horse has had no training to carry a rider, have weight on its back, or pull any kind of cart or vehicle. It has not learned to follow any commands by a handler or a rider.

2. **Dumb broke**

    This stage is where a horse has just started with training. It is used to having a rider on its back and is being taught how to respond to certain commands such as acceleration, slowing down, and turning left and right.

3. Broke to death

This is the last and final stage of the breaking-in process. A horse which is 'well broke' is comfortable being handled, ridden, and responding to all its rider's aids. It is now considered safe for a rider, hired for work, and getting wherever it needs to go with weight on its back.

Depending on the horse's learning style, nature, and lifestyle, the breaking can happen quickly or it can take a tremendous amount of time. The process of breaking a horse can be as short as 30 days or as long as six to eight months. The bond between a horse and the handler who breaks it plays a vital role in how a horse responds to the process of being more controlled and having a rider on its back.

Here is why I adopted this definition. I didn't totally realize I was about to be ridden for the Kingdom, because I kept spitting the bit out of my mouth. An exhausted horse will keep spitting the bit out and will run less aggressively to signify to its rider that it has had enough. It will take the control out of the rider's hand and try to behave its own way.

I was a horse too tired to ride, so I slowed

down spiritually to signify to my rider (God) I had enough. However, the slowing down wasn't working. I would have to surrender and say something. Unlike the horse, I have a voice, and God was waiting for me to use it.

When being broken, the relief and strength you need to continue comes with confession. Pretending to be "all in with God," minus an admission of my exhaustion, was unacceptable. I would have to learn to be honest about myself, and I would need to share it with God. The relief confession brings is paramount if you plan on graduating from your breaking.

Brokenness is a state of complete surrender—it has a character. It's the admission of your imperfections and inadequacies outside the mercy and help of God. It kills a sense of self-sufficiency. You will learn how to say, "I cannot do it without God!"

Brokenness was designed by God to kill pride in man. The person who refuses to admit they are inadequate without God has pride at the very core of their existence.

There are three things you can do in the midst of suffering brokenness.

In the face of it, you can either break out, break down, or break through.

If you break out, you rebel against God—you break out of the boundaries he has set for you.

You run away. You run away from your problems and grow bitter, hateful, and hard.

Or you can break down. There is much of that happening today. People becoming neurotic, being filled with self-pity, running away from life, and withdrawing from society.

Or, by the grace of God, the Christian can break through and accept the suffering with joy, realizing God is using it to prepare you for future glory!

Praise the Lord!

You're more productive if I break you!

~God

Chapter 5 Questions for Discussion

1. Would you say you are broke, broken, or living in a state of perpetual brokenness?

2. Is this where you want to remain?

3. What do you need to do to go from where you are to where you desire to live?

Chapter 6~Who Broke You?

"He heals the brokenhearted and binds up their wounds."
(Psalm 147:3 NASB)

Mephibosheth

As I sat in the drive-thru of one of my favorite fast-food restaurants, this conversation begins with the guy at the window. He seemed distracted as he took my money, because he kept looking at my car. He gazed from the front end to the bumper, eyeing the interior and listening to the exhaust system.

"Do you want to sell it?" he asked.

"What makes you think I want to sell this car?" I replied. "There's no for sale sign on it. Why would you want to buy this car?"

His response was both eye opening and enlightening enough for me to share. "If you've had this car this long, and it still runs this quietly, it must have survived some hard times, and that means you've taken good care of it."

He was right. I've had this Acura TL for 15 years. After a new engine, a rebuilt transmission, and many routine maintenance appointments, it's still in excellent condition.

What got me about this guy is that he wanted to buy it not because it was obviously a decent looking car, but that it had obviously withstood some testing times. Hot summers, brutal winters—including snow 2021, when the temperatures were below freezing for three days and caused power outages all across the DFW metroplex.

Don't get me wrong. This car has broken down on me a few inconvenient times and has had to sit on the side of the road a few hours, but it's still on the road to this day. He, being a fairly older guy, maybe in his early to mid-forties, must have known something of the value of longevity.

I learned over the years with this car that I understand how it works, because I've been the only owner, and we've been in this vehicular relationship a long time. I know all the ins and outs of the car, so I'm familiar with the places it's been broken. This has caused me to be extremely aware of the things that need detailed maintenance and routine checkups.

If I planned on keeping it in working condition, I'd have to be in tune with the necessities and standard maintenance like oil changes, fluids and tires, and of course, the brakes.

The brakes, and the breaks that could lead to a severe breakdown, could put my life and others in danger. I would have to document what has been broken, what's on the verge of breaking, and how much it could endure before it broke again. It's admirable on gas and reliable to get me to my various destinations within the state of Texas. It's not necessarily a long road trip type of vehicle, but it's sufficient enough to be of service within the cities.

What if I told you that you were worth more to some in your brokenness than if you were completely healed and made whole? What if I told you people would be more receptive to listen to you and hear your story if they knew what you had to go through and saw you were still alive and in good working condition through it all? Would you believe me?

I found out that your value is not found in how much you have or how bright your exterior shines in complimentary lighting. The shine of the rims and sophisticated interior aren't indicative of what you can bear. There's a fascination with seeing how you made it through with limited resources. Remember, Jesus died with nothing.

People want to know how you survived after the hell you've been through! That's what makes the broken life the best! The ability to tell where you've been and what you've been through speaks volumes to those who may be struggling in their breaking storms.

This chapter is opportunistic. It gives you, the reader, an opportunity to identify real brokenness within that you never really share. Hidden inside all of us is a brokenness that had absolutely nothing to do with you or the decisions you made. This brokenness was thrusted upon you! It left you with no one to turn to and no one to talk to, and you've been keeping it inside for years now. I'm earnestly praying for you in this chapter. My prayer is that if you've stayed with this book for this long, you are real close to understanding how your best life can only be lived through your brokenness.

Although we never tell everyone about our brokenness, some of it is strictly God ordained to show you and me the real nature of God's amazing grace. One of the wonderful things about scripture is that God has chosen to turn our curses into blessings. He did this through Jesus who became a curse for us that we might inherit the blessings of Abraham (Gal. 3:13).

This comes true in our lives. As we journey through difficult times, God often turns those difficult times into blessings that come only in our future. His promise to us is "all things work together for the good of those who love him, who are called according to his purpose (Romans 8:28).

This theme comes to us in a number of different places in the Bible, and one of the most powerful ways it conveys itself is in the story of Mephibosheth. We find his biblical story in II Samuel 9.

This man was mishandled at an early age, but by the grace of God, his brokenness got him a perpetual seat at the King's table. His life and story show us how to live a successful, broken life, trusting God after losing faith in men.

There was a knock on the front door. Makir went to answer the door. There stood Ziba with an authoritative look on his face in his gardening clothes.

He told Makir the news bluntly. "David wants to see Mephibosheth. NOW!"

Middle-aged Mephibosheth trembled, sitting on his mat in the corner of the room, enjoying the cool breeze from a window. Even in the heat of the day, a cold chill ran through his arms and back.

Finally, after all those years, King David found him. His life was going to end just like his father and grandfather. His life had not been fair. It started out great. His father was Prince Jonathan, and his grandfather was King Saul, the first great king of Israel and Judah.

He was royalty, and royalty had many privileges. When he was young, everything seemed to come his way—the gifts, the friends, the fun—all because he was royalty. Back then he even had a royal name, "Mirab Baal," meaning "opponent of Baal."

Baal was a false god, but his new name, Mephibosheth, meant "Son of Shame." All because of that one day when everything changed.

When he was only 5 years old, a man, bloodied and exhausted, ran into the palace gates and yelled. "King Saul and his sons are dead! King Saul and his sons are dead!"

The same chill ran through Mephibosheth's body that day, many years before. Back then, he did not understand it.

Suddenly, the palace became a place of panic. Wives wept, servants were white with fear.

Mephibosheth remembered how his nurse came running up to him with a few things in her hand as she yelled. "RUN, Mirab Baal! Run for your life! RUN!"

He didn't understand why, but he obeyed. He ran with her as hard as he could, but his five-year-old legs could only go so far. He had to stop. In desperation, his nurse picked him up, and with Mirab Baal in her arms, she ran and ran.

Perhaps she didn't notice the rut or divot just in front of her, and as her ankle buckled and she fell, Mirab Baal flew out of her hands, landing with a hard smack on his back.

Mirab Baal didn't feel the pain in his back right away, and his nurse, weeping, seeing that he looked ok picked him up and kept hobbling on her sore ankle. She had to get young Prince Mirab Baal into hiding.

A short while later, she discovered Mirab Baal was hurt badly.

In exhaustion, she eased him to the ground, hoping he would run or even walk far away. But all he did was fall to the ground.

She begged him to stand up, but he couldn't. His back was broken, his feet and legs useless!

On the day his dad, Prince Jonathan, and his grandpa, King Saul, died in battle, a part of his livelihood died as well. Mirab Baal's life went terribly wrong. He was lame in both feet. His nurse took him to Lo Debar, a city far away from the palace where he would be safe. His name was changed from Mirab Baal to Mephibosheth. After all, who would be interested in a person with a name like that? "Son of Shame."

He had to learn how to live without his legs. Oh, they were still there, but they did nothing. He had to learn to sit again. He had to learn to be carried by others. He had to learn to be cared for by others. And he always had to pay special attention to his feet. They quickly developed sores, and then they took a long time to heal because they had poor circulation since he couldn't exercise.

His nurse continued to care for him, but living in secret, without his dad and without his grandpa, I imagine was hard—very hard.

The brokenness of being dropped has repercussions. It lowers self-esteem and blinds a person of their sense of value.

Who dropped you?

One of the keys to unlocking the door to your best life is to admit your brokenness. This will allow you to move from Lo-Debar to the life you desire.

May I ask who dropped you? We all have our stories where we feel like we're living in a fish tank where we can't be heard and we can't get out. We can only be seen. And when you wanted to say something, you couldn't because you felt the shame of Mephibosheth. Mephibosheth or "the son of shame" can't speak life into his legs, because he feels he wouldn't know what to say. As long as the enemy of our faith keeps us silently ignoring our brokenness, there will be no better life available.

Growing up, we all had someone caring for us at one point in time, holding us in the stead of our parents. They bathed us, fed us, clothed us. They supported our parents in many ways, and perhaps somebody along the way dropped us.

That moment when no one was looking—no

one was paying attention they did something to us that still affects us today. Have you ever felt like you've been dropped?

The person your parents trusted. That senior brother or sister? Granny, uncle, friend, husband, wife… did they drop you? Was it your boss you looked up to?

That person you loved so much left you to love someone else? That person who told you I got your back? Family member who promised to help you in your time of need now won't answer the phone. Someone who you admired promised to help but demanded sex? Someone who spoke well of you in public but stabbed you behind your back? A pastor? A church member?

Sorry to bring all this up, but Ziba is at the door and the king is waiting to see you now!

Mishandled

There will be times in your life when the people assigned to handle you will hurt you. Whether it's an intentional act inflicted or an accidental occurrence, people drop things, and the effects are still painful. There are times when the pain of ministering will mess some people up for life, because those who say they love you will inevitably leave you.

Ziba was at the door. "King David wants to see Mephibosheth. NOW!"

But there was nothing Mephibosheth could do. His legs did not work. He could not run. He could not fight. He could only face the end of his life with honor and go see King David.

Cursed because of King Saul's decisions, everything went wrong for him. At times, he wished he had never been born a prince, but there was no way of changing that. Ziba was at the door.

I want to help you my friend and reader to see that you can live a blessed life even if being broken wasn't your fault. Our tendency is to beat ourselves up when we were the cause of our break, but what happens when the break was someone else's fault? How is the best life possible when clearly it wasn't my fault? Another person responsible for his welfare dropped him.

First, don't get stuck where you got dropped. People who don't find a way to get past their childhood hurts will be left with a matured body and adolescent emotions.

Resting in the arms of a caretaker responsible for breaking you would give me reservations and the feeling of being unsafe in their care.

He was resting in the palace but had to escape to Lo-Debar, because nobody wanted a crippled child. People will have mercy on a broken child but will not show the same mercy for a broken adult.

Can you imagine the emotional state of Mephibosheth?

Misunderstood

We see where he lived, but we rarely take the time to ask how he got there. He's broken, but it wasn't his fault. He's living in a place he didn't choose to live. He can't scream for help, because nobody will hear him, and if they do, they may hand him over to the new king.

Lo-Debar is the place where you can't scream. He would leave if he could, but his feet are broken. He would run away, but he can't run. He would have gotten himself together, but he can't do anything for himself.

So he can't scream, can't run, and fears for his life every second he lives. He's as broken as anyone could be by no fault of his own.

I wonder if you're reading this chapter, broken, but it's not your fault. You've been abused by your mate, but you're afraid to rock the boat and break up the family, so you stay there silently broken. Your kids are grown up now and upset with you because of all the years you spent unhappy, and you took it out on them. You wanted to speak up, but you were ashamed. You wanted to run away, but you couldn't use your legs and feet. Paralysis kept you in Lo-Debar. If people only knew why you stayed, they'd understand.

Maybe you wanted to go to college, but being raised in a single-parent home forced you to work to help out with the bills. You wanted to leave, you wanted to say something, but your service was needed there, so the family could survive. Now you're grown and hate every job you ever had. Failure to speak up kept you in Lo-Debar. You, too, wanted to run away, but you were broken in both feet. Silence kept you in Lo-Debar.

How can you get your life back and live it out better this time?

Try it again

In a strange way, Mephibosheth's curse was a blessing. Because of his broken back and useless legs, he could never fight David as his brother did.

All Mephibosheth could do was hide. He lies there on his mat in the corner of the room, and his life says, "Here is what is left of my dream."

He's totally surrendered by his circumstances. I have to remind you of the purpose of this book. The way to achieve your best life broken is **complete surrender and acknowledgment of your insufficiencies and total dependence on God!**

This posture of yielding was designed by God to be accepted as his sons and daughters. Now the king can look on him with favor and his love.

Trust again

He has no choice but to lay down and learn to trust, because he's lame in both feet.

The only person who remembers him is Ziba, the servant. The best life is given to those who can learn to keep trusting God even when you've lost faith in men, because broken crayons can still draw straight lines. It all depends on how you hold them!

God is calling you to give way to something that gave in on you the last time you trusted. The best life is always experienced by those individuals who are willing to try to live again. Broken doesn't mean you can't live better. Your efforts determine how you live your life. Living in Lo-Debar is still a problem for most people today.

The people who live there choose to make it a geographical location, failing to realize they're making it a spiritual destination. You have to decide to come out.

Mephibosheth's feet weren't working, but his heart was. He made up his mind to willingly be carried in the arms of a stranger.

You might have the question I had about Mephibosheth climbing into Ziba's arms, the arms of another human being let him down in the first place.

The reason you're not living your best life is perhaps you're afraid to rest on someone else again. This is a natural reaction when you've been disappointed. It's hard to trust again once you've been hurt.

Can you imagine the turmoil within

Mephibosheth's heart? "You're telling me to do this pick me up and carry method again?"

What would you have said? What would you have done? Being dropped is how I got here, and I have to do it again? Yes. Sometimes life is better with God the second time around.

Take your seat at the table

The nurse that dropped Mephibosheth made the same mistake we do. She assumed that David came to the door with judgment, condemnation, and death. She obviously didn't know King David, did she?

She was completely unaware that he was different from others. Yes, David was kind. He was noble. He was gracious. But she didn't know him to be this way.

This misconception of David caused her to do what? Take Mephibosheth up and flee from David's presence, breaking her charge in the process.

Likewise, this misconception of God's true nature has led many Christians, when they missed the mark and fell short of His glory, to run from Him rather than to Him. All while running, we fail to miss out on the spread our King has graciously prepared for those of us who trust and believe in him.

When we run from God in fear, guilt,

condemnation, etc., we open ourselves to falling even further into more permanent frustrations and catastrophic conditions.

The Psalmist must have had Mephibosheth in mind when he penned one of the most eloquent oxymoronic passages ever written in the 23rd Psalm. "… he prepares a table before me in the presence of my enemies." What a reminder of God's grace.

Picture the scene in the king's royal residence. Gold and silver fixtures hold the flaming torches that lined the palace walls. Lofty, hand-carved wooden ceilings crowned each spacious room, including the banquet hall where David and his family gathered for evening meals. Once seated, the tablecloth of grace covers his feet. "Mephibosheth ate at David's table as one of the king's sons" (II Samuel 9:11 NASB).

You and I are sons and daughters of God, and as long as we live, we have a seat at his table. So, take your seat and always remember, when you are invited over to have dinner at the table, no one is positioned to look at your feet only your face. No matter how broken you are, you've been covered by his grace!

Everything must be broken in order to live. The seed must break open in order for the tree to grow. The egg must break open for consumption and for life to emerge. The cloud must burst for rain to fall.

"You were never meant to stay in your shell." ~Thomas Lloyd Qualls, *Painted Oxen*

Your life may be broken, but as you reflect on it while sitting at the king's table, you realize it's not that bad after all. It could have been worse.

Prayer:

Lord Jesus, You came to carry on your shoulders the curse for us, so that we could receive the blessing from you. You can turn even the very painful things in our lives in to blessings, you can use them to bring us to you so that we might be restored to being sons and daughters again, sons and daughters to the Lord of the Universe, Father, Son and Spirit. You can restore us to being royalty again! Thank you through Jesus, our Savior. Amen.

Chapter 6 Questions for Discussion

1. Have you forgiven the broken person responsible for breaking you? How do you know?

2. If Lo-Debar is a place to get away and not to stay, why do people continue residing there?

3. What faults do you see in other's feet that you've been covering in yourself?

Chapter 7~Broken Bread

… looking up to heaven he gave thanks and broke them…
(Luke 9:16b NIV)

If you have family and friends, at some point you have been involved in the preparation of a meal for a large group of people. This may have been a holiday meal, a wedding reception or rehearsal dinner, food for a party, or involvement in a fundraising dinner for some organization. If you've done this before, you know the importance of good planning.

Some of the unsung heroes of our church are the ladies who prepare meals for families before or after a funeral. It is a great opportunity to minister to grieving families in a very practical way. I've noticed the family and friends of the deceased are more receptive to receive our service during this time, because they find themselves in church dealing with grief that has left them broken.

The only thing the ladies who prepare these meals ask for is a good estimate of how many people will be coming to the meal. The times when we guessed on the low side have seen quite the flurry of activity in the kitchen and me running to the store to pick up more food.

The disciples of Jesus faced a similar situation in Luke chapter nine. They were probably planning a meal for thirteen people (the twelve of them and Jesus), but instead several thousand hungry people showed up!

Can you imagine the panic of planning a meal for a few only to find out that you are thousands of servings short?

Those who have heard the miraculous feeding of the multitudes story resulting in Jesus taking two fish and five barley loaves and turning it into a buffet in the desert can agree it was a majestic display of his provisions. However, we can be guilty of getting caught up in the miracle and miss the message of how necessary it is for Jesus to break us, like broken bread, before we can live and share this best life with others.

Why is it so important to recognize that the bread is broken? Because we are broken, too!

When Jesus shared this meal with his followers, he gave thanks and then broke the bread and passed it to others to share. At a common meal on the night of Jesus' resurrection Sunday, the disciples on the road to Emmaus described "how he was known to them in the breaking of the bread" (Luke 24:35 ESV). Paul would later add, "And is not the bread that we break a participation in the body of Christ?" (1 Corinthians 10:16 NIV).

What we share goes way **beyond bread and wine**. This breaking of bread is a holy moment and a sacred experience. We would do well to pause and think a moment or two about this bread that is broken and why it is broken.

This breaking of the bread can be so much more than just a symbol, custom, language, and idiom. Something about our brokenness connects deeply to bread that is broken.

We acknowledge our world is tragically broken and enslaved to the power of sin and death. We confess our own brokenness without the gift of God's grace. We remember the brokenness of Jesus' body as he faced his torturous route through betrayals, trials, denials, beatings, and crucifixion to the empty tomb. We recognize the brokenness of Jesus' friends as they saw him die and watched all their dreams shattered.

Praise God! All of this brokenness is absorbed and transformed by the Lord's triumphant victory over hell, sin, and death when he rose from the grave (1 Corinthians 15:56-58).

We celebrate this victory as we celebrate The

Supper as the earliest Christians did. We at New Fellowship Church take the broken bread on the first Sunday of the month.

We break the bread as more than just a symbol and an expression we repeat. We break the bread to remind us that this broken bread is for broken people.

Brokenness is absorbed in new life, new hope, and the promise of a better day!

Living a life of peace in spite of the broken pieces is greatly desired but seldom discovered, because so many people fail to follow the simple and sacrificial steps I found in the story of the multitude feeding.

Living your best life begins with learning how to deal with **frustrations** and **inconveniences**.

When following Christ, remember this: you will be inconvenienced, and you will get frustrated with Jesus.

Three Frustrations that lead to his manifestation

I imagine after watching the clock all day, listening to Jesus teach, the disciples were feeling a bit weary and ready to call it a night, but the need to feed the people who followed took precedence in the mind of Jesus. This was at the heart of Jesus' joy for living his best life broken. He never missed an opportunity to teach and enlighten us along the way, even if it meant inconveniencing himself. Christ will do the miraculous, but He often chooses to involve us.

Jesus says, "Place who you are and what you have in my hands. Your broken life. Your story. Your frailty and your failure, your pain and your suffering. Put it in my hands. You'll be surprised what I can do with it."

Jesus told His disciples to give the people something to eat. They protested they had nothing to give until they searched the crowd. Ready to do the miraculous, he chose to involve the twelve. I imagine the frustration on the faces of Peter, James, and Phillip along with the other disciples. It seems they were a bit argumentative with Jesus but soon came to grips with the truth. Jesus is going to have his way or no way at all.

Your frustrations with Jesus must be suppressed if you are going to experience the abundance the best life can bring.

Can you imagine the consternation the disciples must have felt when Jesus told them to give the people something to eat? He's saying the same thing to you this very moment. Give the people closer to you the pieces of yourself the Lord has kept in good condition and watch how his manifested blessings will never run out as long as you're willing to give yourself away.

Give your story to someone who needs to hear

it. Give your resources to someone who could benefit. Give a helping hand whenever you can, and the divine chef will always multiply your efforts while giving fulfillment that will carry you throughout your life.

Jesus knows that out of our emptiness, He can bring fullness. Out of our weakness, He can reveal His strength. While the disciples thought what was offered wasn't enough, Jesus teaches if we place what we have in his hand and allow him to break it up into pieces, there will always be enough to share with leftovers to begin all over again.

As he broke the bread, it multiplied! He took what was offered, broke it in his hands and gave it back to be given away. As he breaks us, the pieces we deem worthless can now be used in service to all mankind. In another of the gospel accounts, we are told one of the disciples complained it would take eight month's wages to feed this crowd.

Sometimes it's when we don't feel like we have anything to offer that God takes our "not enough" and transforms it to "more than enough."

Your frustrations and inconveniences are servants and tools of your faith, teaching you and me "man does not live by bread alone but by every Word that precedes out of the mouth of God!" (Matthew 4:4 NASB).

We are the bread in the hands of Christ. He first of all wants us to freely offer ourselves and yield to whoever he chooses to handle us. If it's to be broken, then so be it.

There must be separation before there can be multiplication. Anything that is placed in the hands of Christ will be multiplied in the Master's hand.

Patience is paramount

Jesus gives a strange command. "Separate into groups of fifty. This is going to take a while."

I can hear people in the crowd that day saying, "Jesus, do you realize how long this is going to take? We have five thousand men, not including women and children a minimum of fifteen to twenty thousand people. We've got to count out fifty people and separate them, put them over here, and then do it again, and again, and again…"

The people are already fainting, they're already hungry they've been in the sun and now the sun is setting. Why in the world would he take all this time to put them into groups of fifty? Why?

Sometimes the best miracles take time. Sometimes we need to realize what God has for us is not driven by need, necessity, or hunger. You can't rush living the best life now! When God is doing something big in your life, you can't rush it. It takes patience!

You and I need patience more than anything else at this moment. The Word of God says, "You need patience so that after you have done the will of God, you can receive the promise" (Hebrews 10:36 KJV2000)

Living the life you deserve begins and ends with doing things decently and in order. This is what is being fleshed out in this portion of the miracle. Having the disciples put the people in lines and rows would take time, and time, even though a short amount, would seem like an eternity when hungry.

Jesus was putting on display a pattern in their hearts that could never be removed or forgotten. Hungry people are angry people. When a stomach is empty, the wait until the next meal can drive a person crazy. Crazy enough to make bad decisions.

This sacrifice would be necessary for all the followers of Christ who would use fasting as an act of worship in living the best life. Fasting leads to the throne room where real worship can take place! When there's a growl in your stomach, a great deal of waiting and watching Jesus break the bread that's so desperately wanted, worship is inevitable.

If you desire to live the best life broken, and you're praying for it, your prayer is really saying in your heart, "Lord, give me the patience to wait."

Participation for the provision

What do you have? The miracle of the blessed life always begins with what you have. It's not a good idea to focus on what you don't have, because that way of thinking will leave you frustrated and disappointed. This miracle began with a contribution from a young boy who has no name but had what Jesus needed. This little boy's lunch is not just an offering, it's a contribution to the King.

The key to receiving the Lord's provisions is recognizing what you have and offering it to him.

It's ironic they didn't count the women and children. One they didn't count is the one he used to bring about the miracle.

He took it, blessed it, and then broke it. As he broke the bread, he lost count. When he broke the food and handed it to the disciples, it multiplied. The blessing is in the breaking. It wasn't until the bread was broken that multiplied.

It is the breaking of life that produces the blessings in life. Some of the most blessed people went through some of the worst breakings before they lived their best life broken. They know the true value of peace and how it trickles down to those they are in contact with. Those people who make other people happy and joyous are usually the ones most broken.

That's why this book is titled *Living the Best Life Broken*. That which refuses to be broken refuses to be blessed!

The blessings are hidden in the broken places. The more he broke the bread, the more it multiplied. This is a principle of multiplication.

First, we see that something must be blessed before it can multiply. The way our money is blessed and redeemed is by giving our first fruits, or our tithe. Jesus, the One who receives our tithes, is the only One who has the power to bless it so it can multiply.

The second principle of multiplication—only what is given away can multiply. If the lad in the story simply kept the food for himself, it would've never multiplied.

The same principle applies to our finances. When we give over and above our tithe, that's when our finances have the potential to multiply. The breaking produced the blessing.

The breaking of the bread reminds me of how the real followers of Christ who have been broken usually are more at peace and have a better understanding of the purpose of breaking. Jesus multiplied their meager supplies and then turned back to the disciples and gave them the bread as if to say, "I meant it. You give them something to eat!" (Luke 9:13–16 NIV).

This message he gave the disciples is for us, his modern day disciples. We are to be distributing ourselves to others just like Jesus did with the bread. Given, blessed, broken, then given away. This is the process that brings forth the fruit of a life that has been blessed!

What you give turns to surplus

The Bible says the disciples brought the bread the boy offered, gave it to Jesus, and he *took it, blessed it, and broke it.*

He blessed what was not enough.

Five loaves and two fish for five thousand plus people is not enough! The disciples only counted seven things they had available to them—five loaves and two fish—but they really had eight things. They had five loaves and two fish, but they also had Jesus. They had forgotten about their greatest resource. They had the One who created the universe! When you learn to be grateful for your "not enough," then God can turn it into more than enough!

Until you can be thankful for not enough, God won't multiply it. When you have gratitude, He can use your less than enough.

You'll never see multiplication if you're ungrateful.

You'll never see the miraculous if you're not satisfied.

You'll never get the abundance until you can say thank you for the little.

Kingdom blessings always begin with small things and small thank you, Jesus' statements.

Sometimes the things we don't want to give or we don't deem worthy enough are the things the Lord wants us to let go of.

The boy offered his fish and bread and received a return on his investment. He, along with everyone there, ate until they were full! Jesus knew exactly how much they needed, and they still ended up with leftovers. This is because your divine provider never gives you just enough.

His name is El Shaddai-not El-inexpensive. He designed life to have an overflow. He designed your life to be lived in the overflow. He doesn't just want you to have enough, he wants you to have more than enough. He wants you to live life more abundantly, and this life begins with people who are broken.

The broken bread left twelve baskets, because God never takes you through anything where you don't have something left over to tell others about. Twelve baskets say so much with so few words. Twelve baskets left over says, "As long as you follow me, you never have to worry about what to eat."

Twelve baskets say, "I am the bread of life, he that comes to me will never hunger." Twelve baskets say, "I will always supply your needs." Twelve baskets say, "exceedingly, abundantly, and above what you can ask or think!" Twelve baskets say, "Look at the birds, they don't toil and yet your Heavenly Father takes care of them."

What do twelve baskets say to you when you are broken like bread?

Many times we ask God to bless us with more while we are mismanaging what he already handed us. God doesn't give you more of what you ask for—he gives you more according to what you can manage. God says, "I want you to have a structure to maintain the blessing I want to pour into your life."

Can you thank God for breaking you now?

Every time you were rejected or even maligned. When your heart was broken, broken home, broken hopes, broken hip, broken back, broken bank account, broken spirit, broken marriage, broken vows, broken membership, broken promises, broken commitment, broken, broken, broken!

That's a sign God is working in your favor.

He knows how to bless us. The bread didn't become enough until it got broken. It didn't increase until it got broken. The very thing God is going to bless you with is the same thing he's going to break.

You cannot feed anyone the bread of life that comes from your life without a breaking. Your season of blessing begins with breaking.

The bread was given to Jesus by the disciples from a boy with a contribution to the Kingdom, received by the King of kings, BROKEN into pieces, and then given back to the disciples to give to all the people of the world.

If you've been trying everything else to fill that void in your stomach but you're still hungry, it is because nothing can do it but the Word of the Lord.

He kept on breaking the bread. The breaking didn't stop until everyone was filled. That means your blessing will never stop. As long as you can handle the breaking, you'll love living the best life broken!

Prayer for the Bread

Thank you, Father, for this simple meal that means so much to us. Thank you, Lord Jesus, for breaking the bread whenever you shared it. We see so much depth of meaning in the brokenness this bread represents—your sharing our brokenness by being one of us. We ask that the Holy Spirit draw us close to your brokenness through this bread so our brokenness can be healed with hope. Thank you for being accessible to us when we are broken. Thank you for giving us a message of hope to share with those we love who face brokenness in their lives. Amen.

Chapter 7 Questions for Discussion

1. Why do you think Jesus blessed the bread before he broke it?

2. Have you ever felt blessed while being broken? How?

3. What leftovers do you have that you can gather as a result of Jesus breaking you?

Chapter 8~Broken Vessel

"And the vessel he was making of clay was spoiled in the potter's hand, and he reworked it into another vessel, as it seemed good to the potter to do."

(Jeremiah 18:4 ESV)

The Blessing of Being Broken

From ancient times to the present day, there are countless stories of expensive treasures from all over the world that have vanished without a trace. For some, we have no conclusive evidence, while for others, it is clear they existed at some point in history but disappeared—buried in hidden locations or stolen and lost.

Clearly, any of these treasures would change history and refine our knowledge of the past, but after centuries of searching, they are unlikely to be discovered.

Moses' tomb, the Ark of the Covenant, the Dead Sea Scrolls are just a few of the lost treasures of the world with special significance to biblical history. Since this is a faith-based book, treasures like The Knights Templar Treasure (1116), the Lost Inca gold, and the Jewels of King John (1166–1216) are treasures never found that would in no way enlighten our earthly existence or grow our faith in God. To my knowledge these lost treasures would not aid one in the realm of the mysteries of God.

However, the former hidden treasures, the Ark, the scrolls, and the tomb of Moses, would have given the faith walker a great deal to discuss at a small groups ministry meeting. Unfortunately, those great treasures were never found (because I believe God hid them), but we who walk by faith possess a treasure that in God's eyes is much more valuable.

"But we have this treasure in jars of clay to show that this all-surpassing power is from God and not from us." (2 Corinthians 4:7 NIV).

God put his all-surpassing power in dirty, disgusting, and indistinguishable vessels for the world to see, but it is hidden. It's not put on display and set in a window of the most popular cathedrals and showroom floors for others to easily see. God decided to put his powerful light in his people—vessels that would need to be broken in order for the world to see it. How will others ever know the light that shines within is the light of Jesus Christ, who wants to give them the blessed life they truly deserve to live?

This puzzled me until I learned to look through the cracks of my own life. I'd often wondered why good things seem to last only a short time, while unsolicited circumstances and distasteful trials seem to linger for so long. I will admit I no longer wanted the burden of leading God's people anymore. I didn't want another failed marriage, and Lord knows I didn't want to lose my mother during a time when I felt like I needed her the most.

My life was at a place where I got nervous every time a season of peace and prosperity appeared, because I felt as if something was coming that would once again leave me broken.

Who wants to follow a broken leader?

According to the Word of God, every spirit-filled follower does. (Psalm 34:18; Psalm 71:20) How else would the people I cross paths with get the treasure in my vessel—unless it's been broken?

Brokenness is that state of being that defines your true character. Not a burdensome prison, bereft of the joy shared in Christ, but a place of peace behind the beauty of a well-crafted but slightly cracked vessel. It is a sacrificial life yielded to Christ. Therefore, I must decrease so Christ can increase (John 3:30), and this can only be done through a life that has been broken. Who says there must be perfect conditions to live a peaceful life?

Believe it or not, some people collect sea glass (beach glass or broken pieces of glass from people who just leave their bottles on the beach). Initially, the bottles have a purpose, but sometimes they end up broken and float away into the sea. If these broken pieces of glass happen to get caught by a wave and flushed into the sea, it's not the end for it. It's only the beginning.

Tossed by currents and tides, its jagged edges are ground down by the sand and waves and eventually are smoothed away and rounded off. The result is something beautiful. It decorates the floor of the sea and turns into a jewel-like design treasured by collectors and artists.

It's funny how things made for one purpose can end up being used for something totally unexpected.

God wanted Jeremiah to learn exactly that. He instructed him to go to the potter's house in order to get a word that would help his people. As he looked in on the potter molding a piece of clay on his wheel, he learned there was more to life than what he thought. He knew we humans understand the divine just a bit better when we have a metaphor or an image to look at.

While there, Jeremiah watched as the potter made something on his wheel. Afterward, he found it was "shachath" in the potter's hand.

SHACHATH. This Hebrew word means "to be marred, spoiled, corrupted, corrupt, injured, ruined" (Strong's). Have you ever felt that any of these words described you?

What the potter made was messed up.

What did the potter do with this creation of His?

He didn't blame the machine. He didn't blame the clay, and he didn't toss it into the pile of trash. No, he remade it.

He took the same marred piece and made it over.

This is when God spoke. "O Israel, can I not do to you as this potter has done to his clay?" He asked. "As the clay is in the potter's hand, so are you in my hand." (Jer. 18:6 NLT).

THE POTTERS INTENTION is to take something worthless and make it profitable. He purposes to take the clay, shape it, and mold it until it is worthy of someone purchasing the vessel and putting it on display for future use.

The clay is not always pliable. The clay is not always malleable. Sometimes the clay doesn't want to cooperate, but the Potter has to work with what he has been given.

We are earthen vessels with a heavenly treasure! And the Lord is not concerned about your outward appearances. He wants to make sure his treasure can be trusted in your vessel.

To make sure we don't take credit for his treasure, he breaks us, shapes us, re-creates us to prove to the world that although cracked, messed up, torn up individuals, we can get the job done for his glory. The light that shines on the inside comes from a hidden source. Him!

No matter what I would choose, even if I weren't given a choice, I know I would want to be whole–unbroken and beautiful–an honor to the Potter, but if you live in this world long enough you know by now, no one is completely **whole**.

On my own, I am not perfect, without chips or cracks. I am probably more like this, barely held together by personally wrapped black cord of works, not able to hold much of value.

But God!

The two words that forever bring hope.

But God takes me, the cracked me, the broken me, this pitiful piece of pottery that could have been thrown out, and remakes me as He pleases to remake me.

If it were up to me, I would have God make me and my fellow broken pots completely new, perfect and complete again.

God had something else in mind.

In Jeremiah 18:1–6, Jeremiah must have wondered why God told him to visit the potter's house (18:1), but he obeyed.

There, he saw a common occurrence. The potter reworked it.

Like the potter who has total control over the clay, so God, the Potter, has the power to do whatever he desires with the nation.

God is the Lord and always at work. When the clay was flawed, the potter started over with it to make something new.

So does God. The flaws—or sins—of Israel and its people do not cause God to reject them. Instead, God continues to redeem the people. How fortunate we are!

Japanese potters from as far back as the late fifteenth century decided to try something new with the broken pieces of pottery they had. The legend has it that wealthy shogun **Ashikaga Yoshimitsu** accidentally broke a tea bowl he loved. He sent it to be repaired, but he wasn't pleased with the results—it had been repaired with unsightly staples. So Japanese artisans wanted to find a more beautiful way to repair his broken pottery.

Whether it came about in this way, a pottery reparation method began being used in Japan around this time. Although doing away with obvious metal staples, the method did not rely on the idea commonly used today of making damage disappear as much as possible. Instead, the idea was to beautify the very signs of damage, to make the cracks and chips stand out in a new and stunning way.

*Instead of erasing the flaws, it acknowledged and **highlighted** them and made beauty out of the broken.* This method became known as **kintsugi**, a term that means **"golden rejoining" (Stewart).**

The artist used a gold-dusted epoxy to adhere the pieces back together, sometimes replacing large chips entirely with the lacquer. At other times, missing pieces were replaced with striking fragments of other pieces of pottery, creating a new, unique blend.

Once the Potter remakes the clay, he layers the broken pieces. These pieces help you live the best life broken if you handle them properly.

Ten pieces to PROTECT YOUR PEACE

Break up with toxic people

The people you surround yourself with affect the way you think, feel, and behave. Establish healthy relationships with emotional and physical boundaries. Whenever you choose peace, you refuse not to let dissatisfaction, disappointments, and even people control your emotions. When you choose peace and no longer allow people to disturb it, then they'll label you selfish and difficult. Be as selfish and difficult as you need to be to maintain peace. Manipulation hates boundaries.

Stop blaming yourself

Everything is not your fault. Everything is not your fault. Everything is not your fault! You can't always prevent bad things from happening.

Never chase happiness

Thinking you need to be happy all the time isn't healthy, nor is it biblical. Momentary pleasure is much different than long-term satisfaction. Look for ways to build in your future by creating long-term goals.

Test your comfort zone

Avoiding discomfort will always backfire. Face your fears, step out in faith, and free yourself from your comfortable little box. God will not fit in there with you.

Do away with the victim mentality thinking

An attitude of everyone is out to get you will prevent you from being your best. If you blame all your problems on external circumstances, you'll never take responsibility for your life.

Trying to impress people

You can waste a lot of your life trying to make people like you. Be comfortable in your own skin and eliminate using filters when it comes to truth.

Pursue perfection

Striving for excellence is healthy, but an uphill battle. You'll never feel good if you pursue perfection.

Release grudges

Punishing yourself while hoping someone else drinks the poison of your disgust is a hindrance to living your best life. Clinging to anger and hatred reduces your life. Living in peace calls for you to act like an apology was given, even if it wasn't offered. Let it go!

Material possessions

No matter how many more things you get, they will not give you peace of mind. Peaceful people are not minimalists—we just know how to enjoy nice things without feeling like we need them.

Self-reliance

Thinking you can do everything on your own is about acting tough, not being strong. There will be times when asking for help is important. Knowing you don't have all the answers gives you a renewed sense of inner peace.

Our Father, the Potter, is putting broken pieces back together in a way that is more beautiful than before, too. The places where you've been cracked are being fortified with gold. He uses your broken places to bring beauty into the world when you let him form you as he pleases. The process is not always easy, and it's not pretty at first. He puts the pieces together, glues them and then places a weight on top of it.

The weight is designed to do two things:

1. help it bond
2. test its strength

After it passes the test, the artisan highlights the cracks with gold, making a beautiful design that covers the cracks and causes the beauty to stand out!

I may feel like I have heavy weights upon me as I wait for my transformation. But in the end, it will be worth it, and I will be renewed.

"Therefore we do not lose heart, but though our outer man is decaying, yet our inner man is being renewed day by day. For momentary, light affliction is producing for us an eternal weight of glory far beyond all comparison, while we look not at the things which are seen, but at the things which are not seen; for the things which are seen are temporal, but the things which are not seen are eternal." (II Corinthians 4:16-18 NASB)

Question: As one of God's creations, when we mess up, would you rather have God throw you away or give you a do-over?

We've all messed up!

But the Lord wants us to learn today that we spend too much time worrying about the vessel when what's most important is what's on the inside.

WE ARE EARTHEN VESSELS WITH A HEAVENLY TREASURE, and I believe the message God was giving to Jeremiah was just that. God's people are more concerned with looking good than being good! The message of hope, prosperity, peace, and salvation is found on the inside, not on the outside.

None of us are whole. We are a whole mess at times, but we all have these cracks, and thorns, and limps we learned to live with.

Your marriage has cracks, your children have cracks, your finances at times are fitful, and your health can become questionable. Your mind will play tricks on you (if you let it), and your attitude at times is less than stellar. Your understanding can be taken captive, and your motives can get an honorable mention when it comes to being broken.

WE ALL HAVE BEEN BROKEN!

You may feel like you have heavy weights upon you as you wait for your transformation.

But in the end, it will be worth it, and you will be renewed.

Nothing can stop the light that shines from within-Maya Angelou

Shine on! You'll find out that others never see you the way you see yourself. Let it shine. Let it shine. Let it shine through the cracks!

For better or for worse

God uses many images to describe his relationship with his children. He uses a shepherd and sheep. He uses a father and his children. He uses a master and servants, and he uses a husband and a wife.

As a shepherd, he protects us from predators. As a father, he watches over us, because the father pities his children. As a master, he trusts us with his possessions. As husbands and wives, he loves us unconditionally.

To this point, my life attracted people who noticed strength and determination in certain areas. These individuals I speak of (currently members of New Fellowship) wanted to know how I was able to continue serving God on a level that seemed satisfying enough to experience stability, even when others knew I was struggling.

Over the last few years, the reality of keeping the doors of the church open became more real than I could ever imagine. The 2020 pandemic almost shut our church down, but by the grace of God we are still a force in the community!

After experiencing a 50% decline in membership, 60% decline in monthly tithes and offerings, and double digit deaths within the congregation, our church has managed to grow through the rigors of religion and the new style of virtual services the Coronavirus caused.

People are joining again, and we are now being held responsible for lives curious to know how we made it. I must admit there are several reasons, but mainly because the leader of the New Fellowship Church of Fort Worth learned how and when to use and not use his mouth. It happened as a result of being broken.

As a newly divorced man, I spend a lot of time with no one to talk to in those midnight hours. One of the things I miss about marriage is the life-changing conversations that happened throughout the night. This is something married couples should cherish and practice no matter what season of life the marriage is in. However, the silence forced me to do a lot of talking to myself or choose to live through those lonely nights in complete silence. I chose the former.

One thing I discovered about myself in that season is the more I heard myself speak, the less I liked what I heard. Hearing my truth at the sound of my own voice sometimes drove me crazy. Preaching to yourself versus preaching to an audience is painfully productive for self-examination. Happening in those nights of monologue with myself, I learned you can't have a be-true-to yourself-conversation without telling the whole truth.

The bathroom and hallway mirrors don't lie. Me hearing my side of the story from an honest, heart-led view was the therapy I needed to get through this soon to be broken season.

The reality of being alone taught me how to listen. I learned how to take a step forward on this journey with God to spiritual maturity. I now know him as that shepherd, father, wife, friend and Lord and Savior at a level I thought I was on but failed to reach while pretending to be whole. I now possess the secret to living my best life broken. Peace.

Conclusion

A week-long fast. World records. A breaking news story. Awkward silence. Kids' noisy toys. Unhealthy relationships. A baseball glove, horses, glass ceilings, eggs, bad habits and a block of ice are arguably things that are better broken. Ice alone should end the argument end of the story. The best life does not consist of the absence of loneliness, nor is it devoid of tears and troubles.

The best life begins when you completely yield to the molding of the Master's hand.

It is a life that realizes it is nothing, has nothing, and will never amount to anything, lest the Potter of our lives picks us up and sees value in the broken pieces.

Nothing is possible without the Potter, the Father in heaven. No one makes it out of this life avoiding brokenness. From our souls to our fingertips, brokenness is woven into our human experiences.

Brokenness is the most common emotion we all go through, but the least we talk about. We'd rather use filters than deal with the real you.

For eight chapters, if you completed this book, you have been ministered to by a broken man. A broken man or woman has a burning desire to be poured out and used by God to serve others. My way to peace was supposed to be a lovely drive of less drama, no losses, and a minimal amount of emotional distress.

Highly unlikely.

As I reluctantly found out, the life of peace is not attained without several broken pieces of things left undone. Since I've come to grips with this truth, honestly announced it, and surrendered myself to God's plan, my journey can now be lived in peace.

I can't remember the last time I slept all night

without a worry or a care chasing me in my dreams. It has been a long journey getting to this place of peace in my life, but finally, I found it, and more importantly I found out why it was so elusive. I had been living as a hostage in my own home because I wasn't being honest about how I felt or who I was.

Finally. I was in the land of peace, but I didn't arrive here by the road I mapped out on my spiritual GPS. I reluctantly took strange service roads, cantankerous turns onto tumultuous streets, and back roads that led to backwoods, but I made it!

Just because you've gone through something difficult and come out on the other side doesn't make you broken. It makes you strong.

Prayer

I thank you, God, for my seasons of brokenness. It has allowed me to see where and why you stopped me dead in my tracks and see the end of what I would become if I continued down that road. It has helped me recognize all I am, all I do, and all I would desire to be is impossible without you. Thank you for teaching me the appropriate response to my sins, my selfishness, and my insufficiencies. I owe everything to you, and I trust you with my broken pieces. Use these pieces to your glory, for Christ's sake. Amen.

Chapter 8 Questions for Discussion

1. If your life was a puzzle, would you spend most of your time staring at the picture or sorting out the pieces?

2. How many times have you been guilty of looking at your life from the inside out, rather than the outside in?

3. Has your perception changed about brokenness since you've read this book? How?

About the Author

Patrick J. Diggs was born January 10, 1972 and is a native of Fort Worth, TX. Educated in Fort Worth public schools, he accepted and announced his call into the gospel preaching ministry in 2000.

The founding pastor of New Fellowship Church of Fort Worth, he has served as Senior Pastor for 18 years. Pastor Diggs received a vision on June 1, 2008 to launch a project to build a place of worship for the community in the middle of a national recession. By faith, he saw it through. The church moved into the newly erected east Fort Worth facility in November 2011.

Pastor Diggs studied at Southwestern Baptist Theological Seminary in pursuit of a Bachelor in Humanities, and also received an honorary doctorate from St. Thomas Theological Seminary, Jacksonville, Florida in 2018.

Aside from his pastoral leadership role, Pastor Diggs serves diligently in the community with the Read2Win program and on the pastoral committee with John Peter Smith Health Systems. He is a YMCA Faith and Leadership Partner and a Certified Personal Fitness Trainer with American Muscle and Fitness Training. The founder of Temple XII Fitness Ministry, in 2015, he released his first personal fitness DVD, which combines spirituality, physical strength, and overall fitness. Pastor Diggs is a strong believer in displaying a body (temple) that exemplifies faith in God.

He authored two books, *The Trial of My Faith* and *Wisdom from the Wild*.

Pastor Diggs considers it an honor and privilege to preach the gospel and lead the people of God down the path of righteousness. He is personally committed to carrying that gospel across the globe. He believes strong churches are built upon strong families. For this reason, he works diligently to teach men their role in the home and to get more men actively involved in church, ensuring practical Christian principles guide their lives.

Pastor Diggs is a great leader, father to his four children, and proud grandfather of four. He is a pastor, visionary, builder, teacher, author, and personal trainer. As Pastor of New Fellowship Church of Fort Worth, the mission of the house is to live for Jesus, look for the lost, and love others with the love of Christ.